FROM
LIVING
TO
LEGACY

Beyond the Barriers of Mediocrity

Work book

Author
Donelle Cole, MPA

From Living to Legacy

Donelle Cole

Copyright © 2020 by Donelle Cole

All rights reserved, including the right to reproduce this book or portions thereof in any form whatsoever. No parts of this publication shall be reproduced or copied in any form without written consent of the author. For information regarding special discounts or bulk purchases, book signings, writing workshops please make all requests to the author and staff at donelle.cole@gmail.com

Printed in the United States

ISBN 978-1-7341077-1-5

Edited by The Haven Publishing, Minneapolis, MN

Thanks for purchasing the workbook. I believe there are two types of people in the world, those who settle for the bare minimum and those who are bred for greatness. My goal in this workbook is to help you excel beyond conditioned mediocrity. There are many tools and references to help guide through each chapter of my book. You should be very proud of yourself. Surpassing the barriers of mediocrity starts by *empowering* yourself.

In the book we discussed two life choices; merely living to get by, and thriving to build a legacy. There are four chapters over the barriers of mediocrity, Identity, Vision, Mindset, and Emotions. This workbook will walk you through the transformation stages of going from merely living to build a legacy. Below is an example of how

Merely living	Building a legacy
Broken Identity	→ Empower and Fulfilled
Adapting mediocrity	→ adopting mindfulness
Victimized	→ Empowered
Living based on the past	→ ☐ Fueled by the future
Scarcity mentality	→ ☐ abundant mindset
Broken emotions	→ ☐ whole and centered
Aimlessly wandering	→ ☐ intentionality

Let start of what some self-discovery, answer the following questions.

APPENDIX A OF IDENTITY: FILL IN THE BLANKS

1. When I think of identity _____ comes to mind? How does the perception of your identity contribute to your life? Page 9

   _____
   _____
   _____
   _____
   _____

2. Values: What are your values? As stated in chapter 1, who you are is a reflection of the things you value. In life, they are things you naturally gravitate towards.

   Some value relationships, connectivity, growth, character, honesty, love, money, family, freedom etc.

   Things that you value in your life include _____ _____.

   How does your values contribute to identity? Page 11

   _____
   _____
   _____
   _____
   _____

3. Principles: Who are some of your heroes in life? What are some principles they have that influences you to admire them? What are some principles and standards you have for your life? What are some principles or standards you need to develop? Page 13

   My heroes' are _____.

   _____
   _____

_____

_____

_____

4. Aspirations: The difference between those who are merely living and those who are leaving legacies is found in their aspirations. The things that you give your attention towards capture who you are and will become what you are known for. What dream do you want or hope to fulfill? Page 22

Goals that I aspire to achieve include:

_____

_____

_____

_____

_____

Identity shapes your aspirations in very distinct ways. The way you see yourself projects the outer perception of your life. Diving deeper into aspirations what type of individual do you see yourself becoming in the following areas:

Business: _____

Financial: _____

Relationship: _____

Spiritual: _____

Physical: _____

As an example: I can see myself being influential speaking life to others in my business relationships.

<u>Financially</u>: I can see myself being savvy.

<u>Spiritually</u>: I can see myself being whole, divinely connected to all things abundant.

<u>Physical</u>: I have optimal health. My body is full of energy, joy, young, and lively.

5. Authenticity: What do you want others to know you for? When people think of basketball, they mention Michael Jordan or Lebron James. When people think of golf, Tiger Woods is the subject. When people think of you, what do they say? If you need to ask someone you trust.

_____
_____
_____
_____
_____

DEFINE - FILL IN THE BLANK

1. Its human nature to define ourselves based on cultural traits i.e. our upbringings, traumas, past experiences, etc. If you were to design your ideal self what would it look like? List three characteristics you believe capture who you are. These characteristics can be things you find appealing, perform well at with ease, or enjoy doing.

_____
_____
_____
_____
_____

2. In regards to skills you would like to cultivate, what are some things you would like to master that would increase your value? What are some opportunities you would like to pursue but have been avoiding _____?

_____
_____
_____
_____
_____

3. When we fell to commit to ourselves it diminishes our sense of self value. For the ideal perception of what we would like to create doesn't align with the reality of who we are. What are some things you believe you need to change about yourself? What type of hindrance is this placing on your life?

_____
_____
_____
_____
_____
_____

4. How do you view yourself in regards to relationships? Do you have an inferiority complex like the illustration and story of Bantu? Beliefs, situations, or challenges that cause me to feel inferior in society includes _____? Page 13
Write of a moment when inferiority prevented you from growth.

_____
_____
_____
_____
_____
_____

5. I feel most aligned with a higher version of myself when I am ____ _____.

Three words that define me are:

1. _____ 2. _____ 3. _____

Pillar Two: Discover your own uniqueness

I placed some free personality assessments at the end of the book. Feel free to dive into some of the sites and place information in the blanks. There is also a free spiritual gift assessment. How does these results align with your current lifestyle? Page 18

6. Let's create an S.W.O.T. analysis of self.
   Strengths _____
   Weaknesses _____
   Opportunities_____
   Threats to growth _____
   _____
   _____
   _____

7. New information I learned about myself includes _____
   _____.
   _____
   _____
   _____
   _____
   _____

8. My top spiritual gifts are _____?
   _____
   _____
   _____
   _____
   _____

9. Gifts or talents that I am currently not using in my day to day life ambitions are _____.

_____
_____
_____
_____
_____

PILLAR THREE: DYSFUNCTION: PAGE 25

There is a thermometer or inner dialogue that dictates your wellbeing. It tells you:

- How much money you will make
- The quality of your love life
- How educated you will become
- What type of people you will be involved with
- Your emotional health, mental, and physical health.

For this reason you must define who you want to become and fight at all cost to achieve this ideal perception of yourself. Secondly, take inventory of uniqueness. Where are you gifted, what is your talent, hobbies, interest, or what skills can you develop to create more value for others. Third, what dysfunctions are robbing you from moving forward? Is there any pain, trauma, or other behaviors that coming between you and your future self, and next section we will begin to dissect.

10. What are some threats to your growth? Being vulnerable about areas of pain open dialogue to be healed so you can grow. I explained many of the traumas I faced. Let's dive a little deeper into your narrative. Threats, pains, and traumas that have prevented me from growth include _____.

_____
_____

11. Pain can be a beautiful motivator to fuel just what you need to level up? How can you use the things that you have been through to fuel your ambitions to make an impact in your life or in the lives of others?

12. Traumas have the capacity to disarm some of our greatest aspirations. It hinders our progress by mentally freeze framing our mental psyche is a specific type of condition. Seeking healing allows abundance to flow freely. What are some painful realities you want to overcome? What action steps can you follow to address this barrier? Examples : mental exercises, counseling, support group.

PILLAR FOURTH: DISSECT

What beliefs, behaviors, and associations do you have to exchange in order to step in a greater version of yourself? In life, there are many things we have to let go of. In this section, we will begin to dissect these factors. There are three major areas that are included in section of "dissect". Three major areas include:

- beliefs, (leave behind beliefs that prevent you from evolving)
- behaviors, (challenge behaviors that limit your growth)
- Associations. (Evaluate and hang around individuals that challenge your growth)

Cognitive dissonance challenges a person's character which is an excellent source of one's identity. When conflict occurs, you have three options: You can make adjustments to reduce the dissonance, which means receive change and grow; you can have another thought and rationalize the dissonance, or you can fight the urge and change.

Dissect Beliefs (page 33)

Give yourself permission to leave behind patterns that no longer suit your evolution!

13. Beliefs that are most damaging to my sense of identity include:

_____
_____
_____
_____
_____

14. The type of beliefs that I want to encompass includes:

_____
_____
_____
_____

Dissect Behaviors

15. Behaviors I need to avoid include:

_____
_____
_____
_____
_____

16. Behaviors I need to develop involve:

_____
_____
_____
_____
_____

17. Dissect associations:
    People that I have in my inner circle for accountability include _____.
    _____
    _____
    _____
    _____
    _____

18. Values that I need to acquire from my closest peers includes _____?
    _____
    _____
    _____
    _____
    _____

19. Qualities that I want to cultivate from my associations include _____?

_____
_____
_____
_____
_____

We discussed behaviors now we must become attentive to "how" certain people or groups influence certain actions. There are four supreme truths about associations and how they impact identity:

1. We grasp a sense of who we are by modeled beliefs and behaviors.
2. A great deal of our learning occurs through observational learning and mimicking others.
3. Behaviors are tied to what we give our attention to.
4. Memory, motivation and often our actions are directed unconsciously.

Do the people in your circle aspire you to greater heights or do they become threatened by your growth? Are the people in your surrounding providing direction or are they distractions knocking you off course?

Direction or Distraction (Page 47)

Accountability starts with being mindful of the type of attributes that you want to cultivate while also modeling out environments that are conducive with the growth you want to experience. Which associations give you direction and which are a distraction? People that inspire me to level up are _____?

_____
_____
_____
_____
_____

Every Jock Needs a Cheerleader

People that are depending on me to win are _____.

_____
_____
_____
_____
_____

People I can truly rely on for accurate, unbiased, constructive and effective feedback are_____.

_____
_____
_____
_____
_____

Winners Circle & Mentorship

My coach and mentors are:

_____
_____
_____

Spiritual advisor:

_____
_____
_____

Financial coach:

_____
_____
_____

Emotional coach (could be a counselor or therapist):

_____

_____

DESIGN:

Being made in Gods image means that I am _____.

God calls me into victory by modeling behaviors like _____ _____.

What does being royalty mean to you? _____ _____.

Affirmations: Create an empowering affirmation to guide the dialogue of your identity.

> **Adjectives can be found on the last page**

Here is an affirmation I read daily:

I, _____ (insert your name) am an honest, intelligent, goal-directed, responsible, committed, and punctual individual. I am a highly motivated, optimistic, enthusiastic, positive, self-starter. I am a decisive, competent, disciplined, persistent, knowledgeable, creative, resourceful team player, who makes great decisions. I am an emotionally intelligent, confident believer that goes the extra mile. I am energized, have great self-control, a healthy self-image, and manage myself well. These are the qualities of a great winner I was born to be and using them every day. I will maintain my momentum and have employment security in a no job security world.

This will enable me to get more of the things money can buy & more of the things money can't buy. I am God honoring and live my live to improve the lives of others.

Below I want you to write an affirmation that highlights your ideal self.

I am:

_____
_____
_____
_____

I can:

_____
_____
_____
_____

I have:

_____
_____
_____
_____

I choose:

_____
_____
_____
_____

I live:

_____
_____
_____
_____

Appendix B: Vision

Now that we have discussed identity let step into vision. From the chapter we gather that we most commonly associate who we are from experiences and memories. When this occurs we tend to live our lives based on past experiences rather than what we are capable of achieving in the future. For this very reason it's critical that you take advantage of your life by creating the ideal vision you want for yourself and others.

In the chapter, I mentioned George Washington Carver who transitioned his life from misfortune to creating a life of significance through the art of vision. By grasping a sense of who we want to become (identity) we can start to focus on the ideal life we want to create (vision). Chapter one was focused inwardly. Chapter two will focus on outwardly. Let start with some key points.

From living to legacy: Vision

- Know what you love and what brings you passion
- Dive into self-discovery: What activities bring you energy?
- Be specific in what you want
- Write it down and meditate on it daily
- Mark the time of achievement
- Study over your vision while you work your job
- Work your dream as well as your job
- Partner with others who are in pursuit of what you love
- Don't just build your dream, build your reality as well.

Create a vision Board

What if you wrote down your vision, took action on it and it turned out far better than you ever imagined? What if?

1. Let's get the mind open to a little fun. Let's use a little imagination to open up the subconscious mind for a bit before we explore vision.

    Imagine: You are given $50,000 to quit your job for 3 months to live your dream. What would you do? Who would be impacted? How would life change for your family? From the time you step out of bed until the time you lay down to rest what does the day look and feel like? What type of excitement do you feel? Who is all involved in your dream and how are their lives being impacted? Write it all down.

_____
_____
_____
_____
_____
_____
_____
_____
_____
_____
_____
_____
_____
_____
_____
_____
_____
_____
_____
_____
_____
_____
_____
_____
_____
_____

As you write your goals I want you to visualize them already completed. This opens the mind up to the ideal of your vision coming to fruition. In the last section you wrote down three characteristic you believe identify who you are. Write those down below. Page 3 of work book.

1. _____ 2. _____

3. _____

What dreams and visions do you see yourself completing in the future: <u>Fill in the blank</u>

_____

_____

_____

_____

_____

_____

Waking up to a dream fulfilled feels like _____?

_____

_____

_____

_____

_____

_____

Now insert the <u>affirmations</u> of you performing your vision with power words:

Example:

I am <u>BOLDLY speaking to millions across that world changing lives</u>.

I am <u>PASSIONATELY helping others live healthier lives.</u>

I am <u>COURAGEOUSLY writing a phenomenal life changing book.</u>

I am <u>ESTATICALLY changing my families' future for the better.</u>

<u>Fill in the blanks</u>

I am _____

I-am _____

I-am _____

2. Things that prevent me from believing this type of life is possible for me includes_____.

Sometimes we have a difficult time believing what we are capable of creating for ourselves. When this occurs, write down your WHY. What inspires you to wake up every day and fight the good fight? Usually what happens is we can see others becoming successful before we can see ourselves being successful. Also we are more

likely to be motivated to provide for others before we will for ourselves. (If you are extrinsically motivated). If so, write down your vision communicating it to your <u>why</u> as a direct conversation. My why for seeing success in my life is _____
_____?
_____
_____
_____
_____
_____
_____

3. Let's visit some concepts from chapter one. Based on this dream and vision I have for my life, the type of individual I need to become is _____

Example: bold, organized, intentional, open, courageous, fearless, etc.
_____
_____
_____
_____
_____
_____
_____

Personal example: When I started writing a book I noticed that I lacked organization. It's a weakness I have to develop. I aspire to speak to millions in the world. One skill I have to cultivate is communication. I joined Toastmasters, a communication group. Skills and beliefs you have to cultivate to successfully achieve your dream involves _____.

_____
_____
_____
_____
_____
_____
_____
_____
_____
_____

4. Purpose: God designed everything for a specific reason. When you were created in the world there was a void to fill, this void can only be filled with whom you're called to become. Things that stir up my soul to pursue passion includes _____.

_____
_____
_____
_____
_____

5. By achieving my goal _____ will benefit the most.

_____
_____
_____
_____
_____

6. **What drives you to accomplish a desired achievement?** Every human being has something that drives them to achieve a desired goal. Rather its certainty, security, the need of significance, control or other human basic needs, our standards are dictated by what we value most. Things that motivate me to pursue greatness involves_____.

_____
_____
_____
_____
_____
_____

This may sound morbid but what drives me to pursue greatness is death. I have lost so many friends whom had great ambitions but didn't follow through with their goals. They were "jammed" up in life by distractions, lack of focus, and the hardships of life that robs people of their desired destiny. When you can get all of these factors written down you can equip yourself to navigate through these hindrances. Next write down people that excelled in the area that you want to progress in to build familiarity and new neurons in the mind.

7. Individuals that created great lives for themselves that overcame great trials are_____. What motivates you to achieve your goals?

_____
_____
_____
_____
_____
_____

Create a projected future resume for yourself

- What do you want to be known for in the future?
- What is your title?
- What are your skills?
- What market will you serve?
- What impact do you want to be known for?
- What type of image do you want to have?

_____
_____
_____
_____
_____
_____

Create an Achievement list

What type of education do you want?

_____
_____
_____
_____

What type of relationships do you want to have?

_____
_____
_____
_____

What type of income do you what to make?

_____
_____
_____

Where do you want to live in the world?

_____
_____
_____

APPENDIX C–MINDSET MANAGEMENT

Mindset is the foundation of life. The way you "think" governs your perception of life. Since the mind is "electromagnetic" the things you "think" will be attracted into your life. Because of this profound truth, you have to become very intentional about your thoughts.

The first thing in the morning play something positive, educational, and uplifting. I highly recommend meditation as a daily practice to go inward. You have to read and listen to a podcast that improves your states of consciousness and it HAS TO BE A PRIORITY. Everyday society has "information" they want to program you with. To go from merely living to build a legacy you have to program yourself.

There were three very distinct types of mindsets in the book. There were mice, elephant, and lion (Page 94). Describe each mindset. Think about the differences between the three.

      The mice: _____
      The elephant: _____
      The lion: _____

We have to carefully monitor what beliefs are most effective to our sense of development and what beliefs are most damaging to our growth.

The beliefs that keep me stagnant are:

_____
_____
_____
_____
_____

Beliefs that challenge my growth include:

_____
_____
_____
_____
_____

Beliefs I would love to adopt include?

_____
_____
_____
_____
_____

Belief system

How would you rate the condition of the following? On a scale of 1 to 10

Mindset contributes to the following areas of your livelihood. What are some beliefs that you have about the following?

- Emotional health:
- Spiritual health:
- Social health:

- Mental health:
- Physical health:

Cultivate a growth mindset.

What are some groups I can join to challenge the ways I think?

_____
_____
_____
_____
_____
_____
_____

<u>Mindsets that are most destructive to my growth include?</u>

There are many beliefs we adopt unconsciously. Sometimes they are acquired from the environments that we were raised in and other times they occur from influences such as the media, friends, etc. The one distinguishing factor that impacts your life from the life others create is "belief." Beliefs will tell you whether you are "special" or "disadvantaged." What you create is a reflection of who you are. In the next section, I want you to carefully question what believes you have about money, relationships, career paths, and spirituality. Do you feel worthy of having a thriving life? Are there any beliefs that are preventing you from evolving?

- Scarcity mindset
- Victim mentality
- Joneses mentality
- Egocentric mindset
- Crab in the bucket mentality
- Merely existing mentality
- Day to day mentality

- Abundance mindset
- Victor mindset
- Personal Growth mindset
- Pure consciousness mindset
- Community building mindset
- Building a legacy mindset
- Purpose driven mindset

On the left you'll see examples of all of the mindsets that was dysfunctional to my life. On the right you'll see all of the mindsets I wanted to adopt for my life. Make a list of your own and be brutally honest with yourself.

_____

_____

_____

_____

_____

Challenge negative thoughts by writing them down in a journal and beginning to question the "root cause" of the perceptions. Create a thought log to create awareness of the impression you have of yourself and then deposit <u>positive thoughts in their place</u>.

If you acquired the "ideal" belief system you want for your life what would it look like?

What does it look and feel like when you are "centered?" When I am centered I am at peace. I am at a euphoric state where "all things are possible." I am open to the universe. I am grounded in my creative obsessions. I am grateful. I am in love and awe of everything profound. I am unmoved by circumstances outside of my control. Write down what centered in your highest state of consciousness feels like so you have a reference for yourself. This will help you when you have challenging thoughts that contradict this ideal state of mind.

My centered state of mind feels like _____
_____.

As you go through your day ask yourself these questions:

1. Are the thoughts I am having bringing me closer to my dreams?
2. Are these thoughts beneficial to my growth?
3. Are these thoughts producing the results I need to further my endeavors?
4. Are these thoughts bringing me peace?
5. If I am having negative thoughts, how can I utilize them to take ownership of my day?

_____
_____
_____
_____
_____
_____
_____
_____
_____
_____
_____

<u>Mindset Management: Breaking new patterns to create new ones.</u>

1. Conscious mind- thoughts, feelings, emotions: door to governed belief system & logical reasoning
2. Subconscious mind- habits, beliefs, imagination, where memories are stored
3. Unconscious mind: blueprint that shapes who you are.

Your mind is more likely to internalize information at a particular state of consciousness, like seeds to the fertile soil. The best time to program things into your mind is when you are in a relaxed dream state or at a state of inspiration. Higher frequencies of vibration open your mind to new expansions such as being in love or excited to learn something new, welcoming who you are into a desired projected future.

Number one, the conscious mind: focuses outwardly on what you can see. It is the doorway to what information is internalized. When information is perceived as worth to be internalized it bypasses the door into a belief, the subconscious mind. When new patterns become a part of who you are, the pattern is hard-wired into the unconscious mind.

I wanted to break this down to help you create new patterns to reshape the reality you want to create.

Let's say you want love, joy, peace, money, and happiness. Keep your conscious mind open to these factors.

a. Place deep positive impressions around you that reflect this perception. I.e draft a vision board, get a tool that reminds you of these factors like a bracelet or chain.
b. Reflect on positive reinforcements throughout the day to ingrain perceptions.
c. Do this daily to train and rewire neuro-patterns.
d. Maintain these positive vibrations throughout ALL circumstances to make them definite.

- Thoughts plus feelings create emotions (energy in motion) = creates reality

APPENDIX D-EMOTIONAL PATTERNS

One of the contributing factors to overcoming the barriers of mediocrity is being "centered". This takes on a form of "recalibrating" to connect with the source. You may or may not be a spiritual person per se but being grounded in peace despite outside variables is the one thing that can cause you to excel when catastrophe is taking place in the world around you. The internal foundation impacts the outer perception. In this section, we will create a state of awareness.

I have faced depression and anxiety and finding my own serenity has been liberating. Being able to identify what triggers certain emotional states has allowed me to "arm" myself with a defensive system. It has also enhanced my sense of consciousness to awareness. Let's create a system for you as well.

Emotional inventory:

My whole life I had struggled with _____.

Times and environments that stimulates peace for me includes:

_____
_____
_____
_____
_____

Environments that cause me the most stress involve:

_____
_____
_____
_____
_____

The moments I experience the most joy includes: _____

_____
_____
_____
_____
_____

I am most fulfilled when I am doing _____:

_____
_____
_____
_____
_____

Hey spice it up! I feel extra sexy when I am _____.

_____
_____
_____
_____
_____

My petty behaviors tend to show when I am _____.

_____
_____
_____
_____
_____

Get clear on what impacts you and what triggers your emotions.

Situations or traumas that trigger negative emotions involve: _____

_____
_____
_____
_____
_____

Being bound by these traumas prevent me from experiencing: _____

_____
_____
_____
_____
_____

Names of people that bring out the best in me are: (the people that bring out the best in you elevate your higher emotional energy)

_____
_____
_____
_____
_____

I am in my best solitude state of comfort when:

_____
_____
_____
_____
_____

I feel loved when I receive or am performing:

_____
_____
_____
_____
_____

There is always an uncomfortable feeling when you attempt to try something new. Stepping into "uncertainty" invites you into a new exploration of yourself. This often dives into conditioned beliefs associated with certain feelings. As you embark on a new venture, incorporate the "then what based questionnaire" to overcome emotional disruption.

Then what Based Questionnaire

As an example: You're going into an interview and someone recognizes you from a past bad experience.

Then what? *I may have to explain my past and also why I am there.*

Then what? *That person may report a past of negative behavior that speaks to my character.*

Then what? *I will set up a second meeting to maintain my sense of professionalism.*

Then what? *They may decline hearing my response and I'll lose the deal.*

Then what? *I'll have to find another job opportunity.*

Then what? *I'll find another job and continue pursuing success.*

This tool allows us to frame events mentally to acquire a sense of control reducing anxiety. Next, let's discuss the iceberg theory.

<u>Breakdown of internal/external locus</u>

Internal and external locus speaks to the things we have control over and the things outside of our control. The idea is to maintain a sense of bliss regardless of the things going on the outside. As an exercise, write down a few things within your control in regards to a new pursuit and the things outside of your control.

Things in my control are:

_____

_____

_____

_____

_____

_____

Things out of my control include:

_____

_____

_____
_____
_____
_____
_____
_____

If you feel your best, you can do your best. In order for that to occur you have to be intentional about pursuing your best emotional state. Here are four pillars of good emotional health.

Four pillars of good emotional health include:

The four pillars of emotional health are physical, mental, diet, and sleep.

My current state of physical health is: _____.

Ways to improve my physical health includes:

_____
_____
_____
_____
_____
_____

My current state of mental health is:

Ways to improve my mental health includes:

_____
_____
_____
_____
_____
_____

My current state of diet health is:

Ways to improve my diet health includes:

_____
_____
_____
_____
_____

My current state of sleep health is:

_____
_____
_____
_____
_____

Ways to improve my sleep health includes:

_____
_____
_____
_____
_____

Environments that influences good emotional health include:

_____
_____
_____

_____

_____

_____

Meditation tool: When you feel overwhelmed in your emotional state try this tool.

Do a take 5

Focus on the "centered" emotional state that you wrote down. Calm the mind by asking the following questions.

What are **five** things I can see?

What are **four** things I can hear?

What are **three** things you would like to taste or can taste?

What are **two** things you can feel?

What is **one** thing you can smell?

This shifts brain activity from the limbic system and amygdala to prefrontal cortex where rational decision making takes place. This is another heart variation tool to improve will power.

Building your mark

Thinking back to section one of identity: What do you want to be known for?

One new idea, objective, or pursuit I will achieve is:

_____

_____

_____

_____

_____

Are there any mindsets you are recycling that has you stuck on the hamster wheel? If so, what are they?

_____

_____

In what areas are you bound financially, spiritually, mentally, or physically that you need to break through?

_____

_____

_____

_____

How often do you serve others, what are your beliefs about helping others and how can you grow in value?

_____

_____

_____

_____

What techniques do you use to create a sense of direction in your life? Are there any goals you have been procrastinating on?

_____

_____

_____

_____

Are you currently on the right path and moving towards a passion that motivates you?

If not, what exactly do you need to do to get on track?

_____
_____
_____
_____

Have you developed a roadmap that will direct and help to manifest your dreams and calling?

<u>Use this strategy to create a roadmap for purpose.</u>

- Belonging: What community can you join or build that enhances your passions?
- Purpose: What drives your enthusiasm for evolving? What fulfills you?
- Storytelling: How can you contribute to or build up others stories towards a legacy?
- Transcendence: How can you create an eternal narrative that outlives you?

Let's use Jesus as an example: Jesus created disciples. Each discipline was a part of a bigger mission. This mission gave each person a purpose and reason for living. The testament of their lives was a story that carries on forever.

_____
_____
_____
_____
_____
_____
_____
_____

Questions: For Renewal.

1. What books are you reading? How are they challenging your belief system?
2. What seminars are you attending?
3. What type of skills are you developing?
4. How are you inspiring your circle of friends or your family?

_____
_____
_____
_____
_____
_____

1. Is there any area of your life that needs to be made new?
2. What areas of your life need to be revitalized?
3. What type of accountability do you have in your life?
4. How can other individuals upgrade your belief system?
5. How are you managing your time?
6. Will you schedule time to honor God and the call he has on your life?

_____
_____
_____
_____
_____
_____
_____

From Living to Legacy

We all face challenges in life. Some result in victory, while others result in misfortune, either way--- as long as we have breath in our bodies we are all given the opportunity to rewrite the script. What changes do you want to live out from this day forth? Write a letter to your future self! Tell your future self how proud you are for what you have achieved. Highlight some of the most amazing things you have learned. Date the letter 20 years from today.

_____
_____
_____
_____
_____
_____
_____
_____
_____
_____
_____
_____
_____
_____
_____
_____
_____
_____
_____
_____
_____
_____
_____

From Living to Legacy

THE DASH

One thing we all have in common is birth and death. It's something we can't escape. No matter where you run, you're bound to run into it. The beauty of the events that take place between birth and death is called the "DASH" that little symbol that indicates what took place while we were here on earth. I want you to write a mantra, one that will highlight the impact you want to make in your DASH. Let your mantra be a reminder that all things *including you* can be made new:

_____
_____
_____
_____
_____
_____
_____
_____
_____
_____

Remember there are people who merely exist, but not everyone lives. What is life if you haven't achieved the mission set forth for your destiny?

Adjectives Page

- Adorable
- Audacious
- Adventurous
- Alert
- Active
- Attractive
- Admirable
- Awesome
- Bold
- Bright
- Beneficial
- Better
- Broad
- Bon fide
- Charismatic
- Creative
- Charming
- Competent
- Committed
- Courageous
- Determined
- Distinguished
- Delightful
- Diligent
- Excited
- Enthusiastic
- Empowered
- Extensive
- Exuberant
- Electrifying
- Faithful
- Funny
- Flawless
- Flavorful
- Graceful
- Gritty
- Great
- Helpful
- Healthy
- Humble
- Heroic
- Hot
- Intense
- Inspired
- Jolly
- Juicy
- Kind
- Lively
- Lovable
- Massive
- Magnificent
- New
- Ostentatious
- Original
- Outrageous
- Perfect
- Pleasant
- Powerful
- Protected
- Provider
- Pleasant
- Proud
- Punctual
- Quiet
- Rapid
- Responsible
- Revolutionary
- Renaissance
- Renewed
- Restored
- Revitalized
- Sunny
- Stylish
- Successful
- Sweet
- Swift
- Tasteful
- Thoughtful
- Uber
- Victorious
- Wonderful
- Yummy
- Zealous

FREE PERSONALITY ASSESSMENT

https://www.truity.com/test/holland-code-career-test

https://www.16personalities.com/free-personality-test

http://you.visualdna.com/quiz/whoami#/quiz

http://www.testcolor.com/personalitytest/personalitytest.php

http://www.seemypersonality.com/IQ-Test

https://www.funeducation.com/Tests/IQTest/TakeTest.aspx

https://www.skillsyouneed.com/ls/index.php/343479/lang/en/newtest/Y

Here is a spiritual gift assessment

https://spiritualgiftstest.com/spiritual-gifts-test-landing/

Free love language assessment

https://www.5lovelanguages.com/quizzes/

From Living to Legacy

… From Living to Legacy

www.ingramcontent.com/pod-product-compliance
Lightning Source LLC
Chambersburg PA
CBHW071038080526
44587CB00015B/2672